VELCRO ▓▓ COWS : nature's solution to inner-city congestion.

a velcro cow
(nature's solution to inner-city
congestion)

throughout this book i have hidden loads of <u>plankton</u>. see how many you can find in an hour, then ~~so~~ try to beat that record for 5 consecutive hours. record your results in the table ↑provided.
and graph

number of plankton found.	hour 1	hour 2	hour ~~4~~3	hour 4	hour 5	hour 6

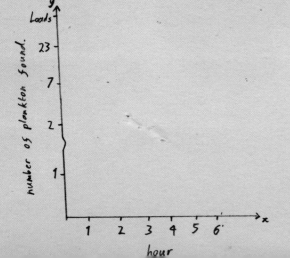

Loads

y

23

7

2

1

number of plankton found.

1 2 3 4 5 6

hour

x

VELCRO COWS:

nature's solution to inner-city congestion.*

by martyn warren.

FRIDAY BOOKS

*allegedly

Introduction

Martyn,

I'm afraid that I have no idea what to say in this introduction thing. I thought if I found some sort of funny anecdote about Velcro Cows I might be able to write something related to that, but despite research in the library and on the internet I can't find a thing, not one single reference to Velcro Cows anywhere! Can you believe it? I'm amazed that you are the first author to look into this fascinating subject, and the fact that all the research in this book is first-hand is even more impressive.

Now that I think about it, I feel that having an introduction by a cartoonist might lead the reader to believe that this is some sort of 'joke'. Have you considered asking someone from the scientific community instead? My cousin lives next door to Dr Raj Persaud, and I'm sure would be willing to show him a copy.

Best of Luck,

Tom Gauld

What are velcro cows?

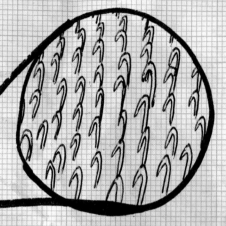

they are covered with
millions of tiny hooks.

Velcro ~~cows~~ look like normal cows.
cows

Where do velcro cows come from?

velcro cows come ~~from~~ from ferries.

5. a) velcro cows, like normal cows, operate via a complex system of pulleys.

How many velcro cows are there?

not many, as this pie chart indicates.

☑ population of cows.

☐ population of velcro cows.

the velcro cow social hierarchy.

queen velcro cow.

fighter velcro cows.

minions.

(not to scale)

on windy days birds get stuck
on velcro cows.

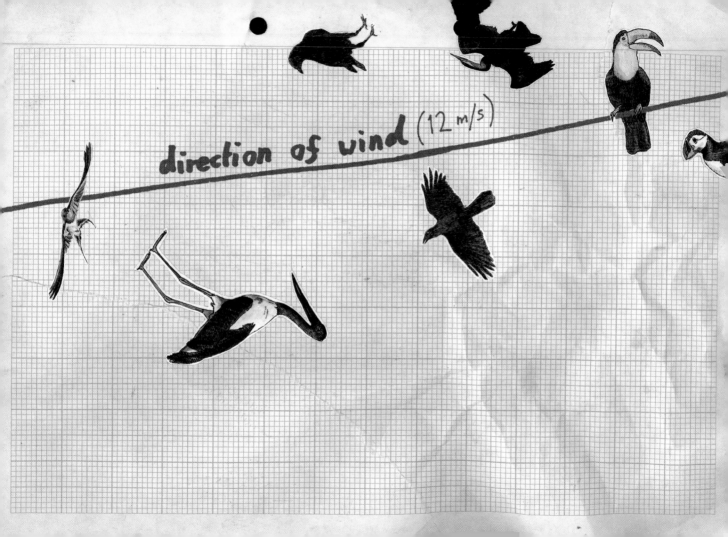

direction of wind (12 m/s)

Q. How do velcro cows ~~affect~~ the water cycle?

fig a. the water cycle.

fig b. some velcro cows.

A. they don't.

The velcro cow food chain.

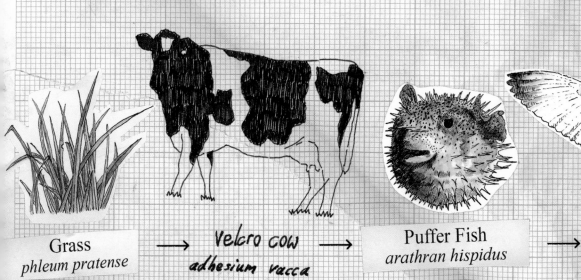

Grass
phleum pratense
→
Velcro cow
adhesium vacca
→
Puffer Fish
arathran hispidus
→
Barn Owl
tyto alba

how the ~~fu~~ do puffer fish prey on velcro cows?

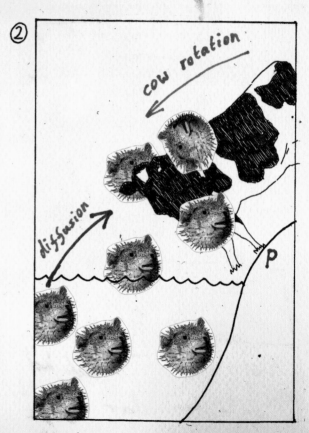

③

gravity

① the puffer fish produce cow pheromones which are released into the atmosphere, enticing a nearby velcro cow.

② when the velcro cow is close enough it causes the puffer fish to move from an area of ~~the~~ high fish concentration to an area of low fish concentration via diffusion. the puffer fish's spiny exterior sticks to the velcro cow under the ~~the~~ adhesion principle. this causes the velcro cow's centre of gravity to shift, making it rotate about its pivot (P).

③ gravity acts upon the velcro cow, ~~causing~~ causing it to fall into the water (H_2O). the puffer fish move against the diffusion gradient using active transport (which requires ATP). with the velcro cow now successfully submerged the puffer fish are able to feast on its flesh. some puffer fish remain stuck to the velcro cow (under the adhesion principle) and they eventually expire due to boredom.

velcro cow experiment #1.

are velcro cows flammable?

yes.

to aid the mating process velcro cows are
magnetically charged.

(velcro cows mate for life due to the adhesion principle.)

Velcro cows are under constant threat from the ~~████~~ v rustlers.

generic sportswear company

X don't do it.

generic sportswear company

the ~~beef~~ rustlers have
thought ⌃of everything.

X don't do it.

famous velcro cows you may have heard of
(or not, depending on which newspapers you read.)

jeremy kyle

henrik larsson

david schwimmer

yoko ono

joseph stalin
(not THE joseph stalin)

sir trevor mcdonald

gillian anderson

bill clinton

chris ofili

nicholas cage

tom roberts

michael flatley
(lord of the dance)

i feel morally and legally obliged to point out that the following ~~cows~~ persons are not actually famous velcro cows;

jeremy kyle, henrik larsson, david schwimmer, yoko ono, joseph stalin (not THE joseph stalin), sir trevor mcdonald, gillian anderson, bill clinton, chris ofili, ~~████~~, nicholas cage, █

tom roberts, michael flatley (lord of the dance).

sorry. .

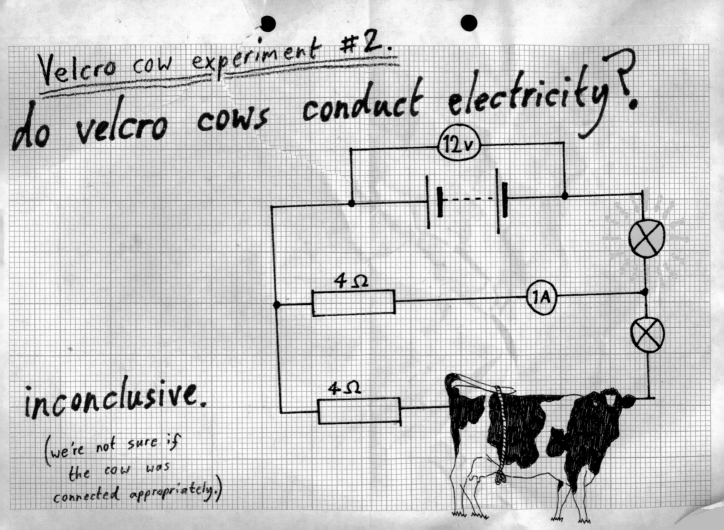

Velcro cow experiment #2.

do velcro cows conduct electricity?.

inconclusive.

(we're not sure if
the cow was
connected appropriately.)

On tuesdays velcro cows are considered to be unpolitically correct, and are censored by a team of ~~dumb~~ government officials.

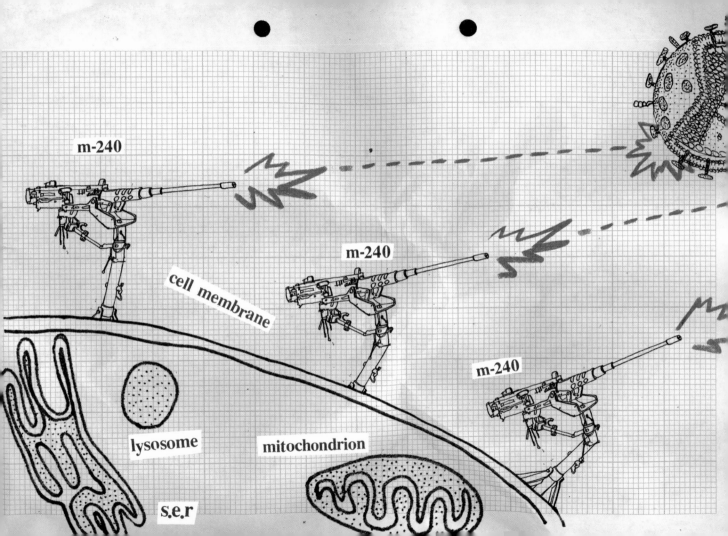

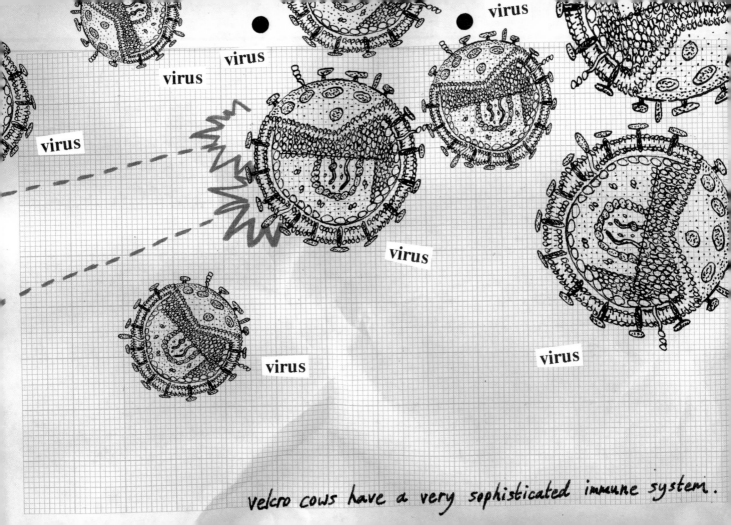

velcro cows have a very sophisticated immune system.

VELCRO COWS THROUGHOUT HISTORY

allied aerial surveillance   5.3.1945

during the second world war (ww II) the nazis stuck cardboard wings onto velcro cows to fool the allies into thinking they had an airforce, or 'Luftwaffe'.

velcro cows in the film industry 1.

Velcro cows
are very cheap,
and don't have
a workers' union,
making them
ideal props for
low-budget films.

velcro cows are so ~~intell~~ intelligent that they are capable of constructing vast, looming citadels.

but they choose not to.

respiration

Velcro cows respire ~~annually~~ annually using
a giant set of external lungs.

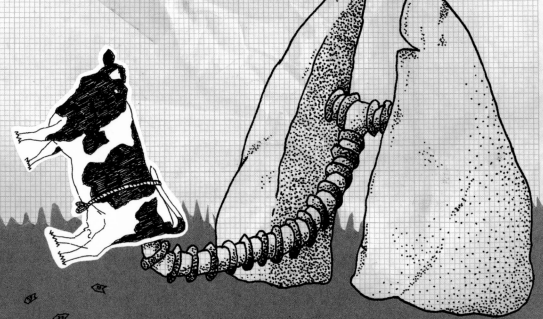

Velcro cow experiment #3.

if you cut off a velcro cow's legs can it still walk?

no. (i don't know what that was, but it certainly wasn't walking.)

velcro cows in the film industry 2

velcro cows'
unique flammable
properties makes
them ideal
stunt doubles
for action
films.

how do velcro cows prey on grass?

① the velcro cow eats a selection of small stones (pictured)

② the ~~velcro~~ velcro cow spits out the stones at an angle of 48°

③ after approx. ~~~~ 7 minutes gravity remembers to act upon the stones, causing them to plummet vertically downwards

④ the stones ~~~~ collide with the grass, rendering it unconscious, and therefore statistically less likely to flee.

likelihood that grass will flee

conscious grass

unconscious grass

①

velcro cow experiment #5

which is bigger, a velcro cow or a cat?

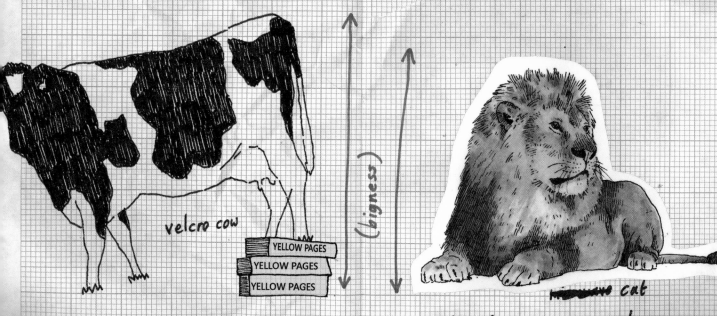

velcro cow

YELLOW PAGES
YELLOW PAGES
YELLOW PAGES

(bigness)

cat

the velcro cow is bigger.

velcro cows like to celebrate christmas in the

traditional manner...

...although they sometimes get a bit carried away.

the velcro cow digestive system:

part 1 - the mouth

(× 10)

Velcro cows have unnecessarily* sharp teeth

*(they are unnecessary because velcro cows eat grass.)

velcro cow defence mechanisms.

Some velcro cows have evolved special fault
lines which are designed to break under
pressure, allowing the cow to escape from
predators.

(special fault line)

~~An Elaborate Hoax~~ An Emotional Plea.

Velcro cows are amusing creatures, and we like to think that you have shared in their comedy whilst reading this publication.
but there's a time when the laughter has to stop.
you see, velcro cows are ~~not~~ in danger from something much deadlier than puffer fish or the ~~generic sportswear company~~ rustlers: STRESS.
every day hundreds of thousands of velcro cows are unable to cope with everyday life (predominantly eating, sleeping and fabricating horoscopes) due to stress. ~~────~~
unfortunately scienticians cannot agree on a likely cause of Bovine Stress Eventuality (BSE), with the most radical theory suggesting that it is brought on by the reappearance of a latent hostility towards a parental figure.
we need your ~~money~~ help.
your generous donation of £7.95* per week will enable us to mobilise hundreds of portable psychiatrists (pictured) who have been trained since birth to deal with an outbreak of BSE.
thankyou.

*non-negotiable.

YES! i agree to willingly donate £7.95 per week to the Bovine Stress Eventuality Awareness Committee and Action Team (BSEACAT)*

name..........

bank details...........

☐ i will allow BSEACAT to send me irrelevant information that doesn't relate to velcro cows or their affiliates.

has a velcro cow ever encountered an inflatable goose?

once. it was a bit awkward.

homework

Answer the following questions using words and ~~junk~~ sentences...

a) what are inflatable geese?

b) what is inflation potential?

c) why do inflatable ~~big~~ geese migrate?

d) do inflatable geese have DNA?

a) how elastic are inflatable geese?

b) ~~━━ ━━ ━━━━━ ━━ ━ ━ ━━~~

c) how are inflatable geese linked to ken livingstone?

d) what do inflatable geese do with discarded jam

   jars?

a) what happens if an inflatable goose is added to a

   beaker of copper (II) sulphate solution and heated

   gently for 20 minutes?

INFLATABLE GEESE:
like ~~old~~ pigeons, but wetter.

- by Martyn Warren

recommended reading ↑

(for additional information visit www.velcrocows.co.uk)

first published in Great Britain in 2007 by Friday Books
an imprint of The Friday Project Limited

83 Victoria Street, London SW1H 0HW

www.thefridayproject.co.uk

www.fridaybooks.co.uk

printed by MPG Books Ltd.

ISBN - 13   978 - 1 - 905548 - 62 - 0

British Library Cataloguing in Publication Data

A catalogue record for this book is available from the British Library

The Publisher's policy is to use paper manufactured from ~~reading machines~~ sustainable sources

www.velcrocows.co.uk

a graph showing the amount of thanks that various people deserve.

Y — Amount of thanks

- many x thanks
- 2 x thanks
- thanks.5
- thanks
- 0

X — Various people

clare christian
clare weber
paul carr
scott pack
heather smith
everyone else at tfp
dereck rogers
pete lloyd
paul osborne
ceri amphlett
jonny hannah
tor freeman
tom gauld
steven appleby
corinne female
tom roberts
sam smith
jenny robins
everyone else at southampton solent uni
the male (+ baker) clan
the cineworld gang
tony blair

make your own... velcro cow conversation.

about the author...

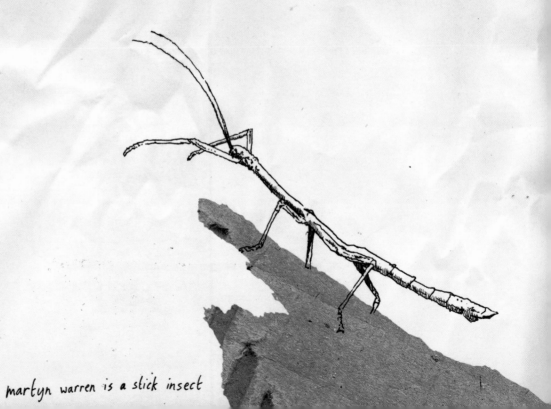

martyn warren is a stick insect